The President Pardons Godot

Books by Nathaniel Hutner

Heracleitus Under Water   1988

War: A Book Of Poems   2003

The Name We Never Lose   2019

The Complete Poems of Nathaniel Hutner   2021

☙

Plays by Nathaniel Hutner

Godot Arrives

Godot Imagine Godot

Godot at Night

Godot, Alive or Dead

The President Pardons Godot

☙

Short Plays by Nathaniel Hutner

Hot Potatoes

The Fix

Keewaydin Plays

The President Pardons Godot

⽷

A Comedy by Nathaniel Hutner

Burlington, Vermont

A collected edition of Nathaniel Hutner's plays, *The Collected Plays of Nathaniel Hutner*, is available from Onion River Press, 191 Bank Street, Burlington, VT 05401

Copyright © 2021 by Nathaniel Hutner

All rights reserved. No part of this publication may be reproduced, distributed, or transmitted in any form or by any means, including photocopying, recording, or other electronic or mechanical methods, without the prior written permission of the publisher, except in the case of brief quotations embodied in critical reviews and certain other noncommercial uses permitted by copyright law.

Onion River Press
191 Bank Street
Burlington, VT 05401

ISBN: 978-1-949066-92-0

Library of Congress Control Number: 2021914398

Designed by Jenny Lyons, Middlebury VT

The President Pardons Godot

CAST OF CHARACTERS

A AND B: The Two Apostates

MADAME GODOT: Wife of Godot

GODOT: Himself

DANIEL: Son of A, B, Madame, and Godot

PRESIDENT (aka JACK): The former President of the United States

LANCELOT BROWN: Psychiatrist, then President

LADY DALY: His wife and former patient (Later: Aide 1)

DOTTIE: Patient (Later: Aide 2)

LUCILLE: Patient

ALICE: Patient

UNCLE STURTEVANT: Patient

DR. FISH: Resident in Vermont

LIZ: Daniel's girlfriend

ANTONIO: Bartender

ACT I

SCENE 1

A desolate wasteland near the Outer Hebrides.

    A
Did he ever beat you?

    B
Beat me? I beat myself. Everyday.

    A
It's a pleasure?

    B
Yes.

    A
Can you teach me?

    B
We don't have time.

    A
I thought we had eternity.

    B
We are waiting on a tea date.

    A
A what?

                B
We have invited someone to tea.

                A
Here?

                B
It will help us get along.

                B
Who's coming?
(B looks upstage to northern horizon)

                B
I see her now!

                A
Who?

                B
Our guest. Madame Godot.

                A
Madame?

                B
The wife of our friend.

                A
That one…

                B
His wife.

                A
And she's coming now?
(MADAME enters)

                B
Bonjour, Madame.

MADAME
Enchanted.

A
Me, too.

B
And me.

A
Should we speak French?

MADAME
I speak English.

A
Thank Heavens.

MADAME
You must be American.

A
(To MADAME GODOT)
Can I call you Ma'am? This is not France.

MADAME
You can call me anything you like. Most names will fit, and almost every history.

A
We must get to know you better.

MADAME
That is why I am here.

B
What about your husband, Godot?

MADAME
He is dressing.

             B
Oh.

             A
Getting ready for his entrance?

           MADAME
Not at all. He dresses to please himself, and sometimes the result is spectacular.

             B
Yes.

             A
We know.

             A
(Continuing to B)
   I could have told you.

             B
(To MADAME)
   I have met your husband.

           MADAME
Many people have, only they don't know it.

             B
He is a bit of a jongleur.

             A
What?

             B
Magician. I rather like it when he levitates.
(To MADAME)
   Maybe he could teach us…

           MADAME
I'll pass on the request.

B
We don't want to presume…

A
Oh, no.

MADAME
No problem. He'd be delighted to teach someone something. After all these years, I am certain he would welcome you as pupils.

A
I make a good pupil. I always did well at school, especially in kindergarten.

B
What did you do in kindergarten?

A
Slept, mostly.

MADAME
Dreams are fun.

B
Yes.

A
I remember closing my eyes very tight and seeing a large red ball of light.

B
And then the light went out.

A
I met you.

B
You opened your eyes.

A
You opened my eyes.

B
I am trying.
(Turns to MADAME)
Have you ever seen the sunrise in the Outer Hebrides?

MADAME
This is the first time I have come here.

A
We hope to see more of you.

B
It's not so bad.
(The earth shakes. MADAME looks alarmed)

A
Just a little earthquake. To liven up eternity.
(B frowns at A)

MADAME
I didn't know the earth could shift here.

A
It does everywhere, sooner or later, but here it's pretty minimal.

B
Just enough to open your eyes.

A
Make you gasp. Not much is going on, otherwise.
(There is another shake)

B
Where is Godot?

A
Yes.

MADAME
He should arrive in a moment.

A
(Quietly to B)
Isn't she a bit stiff?

B
(Quietly to A)
She's French.

A
Ah. Bien entendu.

B
Madame, do you have any children?

MADAME
(Astonished)
Too many, I think.

A
(To B)
We are prime suspects.

B
(To MADAME)
Then all humanity?
(MADAME nods)

B
Oh.

A
It's no good being a Unitarian any more.

           B
Do you recommend one religion over another?

           MADAME
You should ask my husband. He leads, at least he leads me.

           B
Then you are not a feminist?

           MADAME
Not yet.

           A
Even with a husband?

           B
(To A)
You have me.

           A
Ah.
(DANIEL enters)

           B
Here comes our own child.

           DANIEL
(To MADAME)
I am Daniel.

           MADAME
You are one of my favorite children.

           DANIEL
But A and B are my parents.

           B
By adoption.

           DANIEL
Then…

A
It looks like it.

DANIEL
Where have you been?

MADAME
I am a working mother.

A
She hasn't been working on you.

B
Here's your chance.

MADAME
Daniel, I am, in fact, your mother.

DANIEL
Then who is my father?
(GODOT enters)

GODOT
Hello.
(Everyone freezes. DANIEL looks crushed)

DANIEL
You're my father?
(GODOT smiles)

DANIEL
What about our affair?

GODOT
Love is almost as varied as creation.

A
This is beginning to sound like the Greeks.

DANIEL
So you cast yourself as Zeus?

MADAME
He is not Zeus, and I am not Hera.

DANIEL
Do I have to share you with her?

A
Is that your only problem?
(There is a silence)

MADAME
In any case, I do not mind. Daniel loves his father, and that is correct.

DANIEL
At least we haven't slept together.

MADAME
Why not? I doubt you two could produce any children.

B
(Hinting)
What about the taboo?

GODOT
Taboo?

A
Incest?

MADAME
Many people are far more familiar with my husband than that.

GODOT
They eat me for dessert.

A
They don't seem to know it.

B
Should we consider ourselves pantheists?

GODOT

Consider yourselves whatever you like. The facts are the facts. And Daniel is our son. As for our affair, it has gone up and down, like everything else in these matters. I believe we have been intimate, and there were no unfortunate results. In fact, our intimacy confirmed our love. And I don't know that your taboo applies to the relation between two males.

B

Perhaps we should resurrect Socrates and get him to examine the subject.

A

It's a new one.

GODOT

I don't see anything new in it.

DANIEL

You don't?

GODOT

You know who I am. Everyone here is my child, even my wife. For me, your taboo is either universal or irrelevant. I prefer to think the latter, at least when I am with you.

(DANIEL feels a little better)

GODOT

Anyway, there is no reason to quarrel.

A

It's a family quarrel.

GODOT

I suppose.

DANIEL

But what about us?

MADAME
What about me? Have you no love left for your mother?

DANIEL
But this is the first time I have ever met you.

GODOT
You'll just have to get to know each other.

DANIEL
But I have never loved a woman.
(A, B, and GODOT raise eyebrows)

MADAME
Here I am.

DANIEL
I am not Oedipus.

GODOT
And I am not Socrates. Your mother loves you particularly, just as I do, and if you don't want to sleep with her, that shows good judgment. You are nevertheless entitled - encouraged - to love her as your mother. Once you get to know her, you will see.

MADAME
Are men and women so different that you cannot love both?
(DANIEL is at a loss)

B
Life is hard. I recommend you get a job. It will take your mind off all this and maybe even let you redirect your attention to a nice girl your own age.
(DANIEL sputters)

A
Girls aren't that awful.

DANIEL
How do you know?
(B nudges A)

DANIEL
Well?

B
I think life offers us all many possibilities. It is up to you to look at them. Not one of us is entirely like any other, so we will not try to force you to do anything against your own nature.

A
But we do encourage you to explore.

DANIEL
After Godot, what comes next?
(GODOT and MADAME smile)

GODOT
It is your task to find out.

MADAME
And we will encourage you to do so.
(DANIEL looks a little disappointed)

A
Such is life.

B
Daniel, we are all here to help, though I suppose Godot and his wife have a great deal of other things to think about.

GODOT
Daniel, your mother and I are always here to accept your love, and we return it.

MADAME
Where is our tea?

GODOT
Tea?

MADAME
We were invited to tea.

A
That's my job. Come along. I'll get you your tea. It will settle the situation.

(They all exit stage right)

ACT I

SCENE 2 - THE TEA PARTY

Lights up on GODOT, MADAME, A, B, and DANIEL sitting around a low table covered with the paraphernalia of tea. They drink and converse alternately as the scene progresses.

        GODOT
(Pouring)
  Such good tea. What is it called?

        A
  Lapsang Souchong.

        B
  A bit smoky.

        A
  Our favorite

        GODOT
  It is very good.

        MADAME
  It reminds me of China.

        GODOT
  I almost died there once.

MADAME
It was during our visit in the sixties.

GODOT
I was very ill, and news got out that I had died.

MADAME
It created a sensation in America. Godot made the cover of Time.

GODOT
Then we moved on to Japan.

MADAME
The topography in Japan is smilier to this, at least in the north.

GODOT
We always seem to end up in the north.

MADAME
The Japanese reporters asked us about our health.

GODOT
I told them I was dead.
(GODOT and MADAME smile)

MADAME
Memories.

GODOT
Yes. The reporters were not amused.

MADAME
They were responsible for the story in the first place.

GODOT
I had the great pleasure of reading my own obituaries.

MADAME
He was amused.

GODOT
They were not accurate.

MADAME
Very flattering, but not accurate.

GODOT
These days people say the situation is reversed. Not only am I quite alive, some people say I am alive in the White House.
(Everyone laughs)
(A figure dressed like Abraham Lincoln appears in the shadows upstage behind the backs of the others)

GODOT
Yes, the White House.

DANIEL
Have you ever been in the White House?

GODOT
Only incognito.

MADAME
You see…

GODOT
I try not to interfere…

MADAME
He is aloof…

GODOT
I must maintain the possibility of freedom for everyone, so I do not interfere.

MADAME
He encourages.

GODOT
I try to set an example.

MADAME
He does not -

GODOT
I do not dictate.

MADAME
He wishes to encourage individual responsibility.

GODOT
Free choice.
(Black figure steps forward. It is the PRESIDENT)

PRESIDENT
Who are you?

GODOT
Who are you?

PRESIDENT
I am the President.

DANIEL
Of what?

PRESIDENT
The United States.

DANIEL
Of America?

PRESIDENT
Are there any others?

GODOT
Not yet.

MADAME
Would you care for some tea?

A
It is Lapsang Souchong.

B
From China.

MADAME
Yes. It is very good.

PRESIDENT
Decaffeinated?

A
Don't worry, it won't keep you awake.

B
(Making conversation)
Mr. President, what have you been doing lately?
(PRESIDENT is silent)

MADAME
Milk?
(PRESIDENT nods)

MADAME
Sugar?
(PRESIDENT signals no)

PRESIDENT
I do love sweets, but my doctors have taken me off them.

GODOT
Too bad.

PRESIDENT
Thank you.

MADAME
The milk is nice.

B
So, how does it go in Washington?

A
Comme ci, comme ça?

PRESIDENT
We are at war.

MADAME
There is always a war somewhere.
(Pointing to teacups)
Which one is yours?

PRESIDENT
It is not my war. The enemy brought it on themselves.

MADAME
They always do. It is so tiresome.

PRESIDENT
Try being President.

GODOT
I once knew a President who was on perpetual vacation. He played at being President. He enjoyed it.
(There is a silence)

GODOT
He even played at war, when he was not playing golf.
(The PRESIDENT is visibly stiffening)

MADAME
I am certain you are a more serious President than that one, n'est-ce pas, Mr. President?

PRESIDENT
Who are you people, and what am I doing here?

GODOT
I think you are out of office.

B
Something happened.

MADAME
I should have introduced us. I am Madame Godot, this is my husband, Monsieur Godot, then we have A and B
(A and B nod)
and their adoptive son, Daniel.

PRESIDENT
Out of office?

GODOT
Shall I tell him?

DANIEL
You are dead. We are all dead.

PRESIDENT
Nonsense. What is this place?

MADAME
Be civil. And you are dead.

GODOT
You are in the Outer Hebrides.

PRESIDENT
Where are my aides?

MADAME
Isn't it obvious?

GODOT
They are alive. You are not.

PRESIDENT
This is unbearable. I want my aides.
(Tea drinkers raise their eyebrows)

GODOT
Don't you know?

PRESIDENT
Know what?

GODOT
You have been assassinated.

PRESIDENT
You are all crazy. How do I get out of here?

DANIEL
I can show you a way out.

GODOT
There is a cliff a little south of here…

PRESIDENT
(Breaking down)
Am I really dead?

MADAME
That's what the newspapers say.

PRESIDENT
But they only print what they hear from me.

GODOT
The Truth.

B
From you and your aides, too.
(PRESIDENT closes his eyes, then opens them)

GODOT
It is not a dream and you are still here.

PRESIDENT
How do I get back?

DANIEL
You like golf that much?

PRESIDENT
Well, it's the thing everyone... who are you?

DANIEL
Daniel. Adopted and not.

A
(Whispering to B)
Maybe we should adopt the President.

B
(To PRESIDENT)
Would you like us to adopt you?

PRESIDENT
What for?

GODOT
We could teach you how to play golf without walking.

DANIEL
We could give you quite a ride.

A
I used to play golf, and this is Scotland.

B
Maybe we could arrange something, a game with professionals.

A
There are many specialists up here in the Outer Hebrides.

PRESIDENT
I hate golf.
(There is silence)

MADAME
More milk?

GODOT
More tea?

PRESIDENT
I don't much care for tea.

GODOT
We knew that.

MADAME
Here, we drink tea all the time.

GODOT
Anywhere we go: China, Japan.

A
The Outer Hebrides.

PRESIDENT
I can't be dead.
(There is silence)

PRESIDENT
Who killed me?
(There is silence)

PRESIDENT
Who…

GODOT
Your daughters.

PRESIDENT
That is lunacy. I told them never to visit me in the White House.

DANIEL
What about the ranch?

PRESIDENT
The ranch? I think I remember something.

(Everyone begins to smile, except the PRESIDENT who is cogitating)

        GODOT
(Quietly)
Let him think.

        PRESIDENT
I think I remember an accident.

        B
It was not an accident.

        PRESIDENT
But where are my daughters?

        MADAME
What does it matter? They are there…

        B
…and you are here.

        A
With us.

        GODOT
Have some more tea.

        MADAME
Tea has symbolic value: it stands for Truth.

        PRESIDENT
Oh.

        MADAME
Would you care for some more?

        PRESIDENT
Truth?

GODOT
It's a little dicey, isn't it?
(PRESIDENT is silent)

PRESIDENT
How much money do you want?
(Everyone laughs, except the PRESIDENT)

GODOT
People are always offering me things.

B
Money...

DANIEL
Youth...

MADAME
Labor...

A
Attention...

GODOT
Prayers...

PRESIDENT
How much? I have a lot.

GODOT
Mr. President, look into your soul. Do you see any money there?

DANIEL
Now you are pure soul, like the rest of us.

MADAME
Have some more tea.

GODOT
Soul can be very expensive.

(Pausing)
It can cost you your life.

A
B and I discovered our souls before we died.

B
Then we didn't need much money.

A
And here we are.

B
With you.

GODOT
In the Outer Hebrides.

MADAME
With you.

PRESIDENT
I'll give you anything you want. You can be Secretary of State.
(There is silence)

PRESIDENT
I'll recommend you as my successor.
(There is big silence)

GODOT
I don't think I want anything from you, Mr. President, except, perhaps, the truth.
(The PRESIDENT is getting really desperate)

PRESIDENT
Mr. Godot, I pardon you. I pardon all of you.

GODOT
We do not need your pardon, Mr. President. We have done nothing wrong.

MADAME
We would like to pardon you, Mr. President.

A
Just for form's sake, Mr. President.

B
As a matter of course.

A
Even though we are all dead.

B
It hardly makes any difference now.

A
To the world.

B
Yes, to the world.

A
But we still have our future time together to consider.

B
Yes.

GODOT
So we pardon you, too, Mr. President.

MADAME
And we thank you for taking such good care of us.

GODOT
Consult your soul, Mr. President. What do you really want?

PRESIDENT
I want to go home.
(PRESIDENT breaks down in tears)

GODOT
I have heard that so many times, mostly from the mad.

MADAME
All those psychiatric wards, full of pain.

GODOT
They only wanted to go home.

MADAME
And there was no home.

GODOT
No.

A
No.

B
No.

DANIEL
No.

MADAME
(Brightly)
And now we are here.

PRESIDENT
You say my daughters killed me? How could they? I loved them.

GODOT
Mr. President, you are very green.

B
Very fit for a tragedy.

GODOT
And now you have had your tragedy.

B
And you can't take it.

GODOT
You will. You will learn.

MADAME
We all learn.

DANIEL
We all learn.

A
We all suffer, one side of life or the other.

GODOT
Death is a great teacher. Very powerful. More powerful than you, Mr. President.

MADAME
How many people have you killed, Mr. President, I mean besides yourself?

PRESIDENT
But I didn't kill myself.

GODOT
Yes, you did. You may think you didn't, but you did.
(PRESIDENT gets up and begins to walk away)

DANIEL
Where are you going, Mr. President?
(PRESIDENT moves a bit further away)

PRESIDENT
If this is death, you are welcome to it. I am going home. To Washington. I am the President. I must find my aides. I am at war. I am responsible. I am the most powerful man on the face of the earth. My daughters love me. My wife is waiting for me. Always.

GODOT
Yes. You are the Defender of Freedom. Wherever you go. Well,

don't let us stop you. You may walk back to Washington.

MADAME
The long way round.

DANIEL
You can start by acquiring an education. Like me. There is always time to get an education.

MADAME
We all have oodles of time.

GODOT
Why in a rush, Mr. President? If you go back, you will find that time has left you behind. No one wants you back. They have moved on.

DANIEL
Now it is your turn to move on, Mr. President.

MADAME
May we call you "Jack?" "Mr. President" is so cumbersome – and out of date.

GODOT
It no longer applies.

A
Let bygones go by.

PRESIDENT
I feel very tired.
(PRESIDENT tries to sit on the ground)

PRESIDENT
Do you have an extra chair? Jack?

DANIEL
Take mine. I can stand.

GODOT
(Smiling)
I'm sure you can.
(To PRESIDENT)
Please. You are our guest.

PRESIDENT
May I have some more tea?

MADAME
Of course.
(PRESIDENT sips tea)

PRESIDENT
It is hot.

GODOT
It always is, especially up here, we feel it, in the rain and wind, on the heath.

MADAME
If you will.

PRESIDENT
You call me Jack?

MADAME
Or "Jacques." We are diplomats, along with everything else, and French is still the language of diplomacy.

PRESIDENT
I'll take "Jack."

GODOT
Fine. How's your tea?

JACK
I've never had this before. What do you call it?

MADAME
"Lapsang Souchong." It comes from China.

JACK
It tastes of smoke.

MADAME
It is famous for that.

GODOT
It is famous for a lot of things.

DANIEL
So are all of us —

A
— Now.

B
Yes.

GODOT
Well, we have done our good deed of the day.

JACK
What are you all doing?

GODOT
You need some sleep.

A
Or at least a rest.

MADAME
Tea time can be very tiring.

A
All that conversation.
(JACK has already fallen asleep)
(Lights fade to penumbra. Actors freeze on stage)
(BLACKOUT)

ACT II

SCENE 1 – The President's Dream

We are back at the Budinger Foundation. There are chairs on stage arranged in a semicircle facing the audience, enough to seat everyone in the scene. At center of chairs sits the PRESIDENT, wrapped in a straightjacket. Each actor, when speaking, stands. Staff and Patients are indistinguishable from each other, though this appearance is not maintained when someone speaks.

    DR. BROWN
(Banging on the floor to bring the meeting to order)
Quiet, everyone! I being our community meeting today with sad news: My friend Mr. Godot was found drowned on the Isle of Palms near Charleston, South Carolina yesterday.

    PRESIDENT
Hooray! He was a troublemaker and a liberal. We had him under surveillance all through his phony convalescence.

    DR. BROWN
Please. Godot was a good man. Tortured by his dreams, but principled in any case.

    LADY DALY
(Very downcast)
It is too bad.

GODOT
Yes. I loved myself.

DOTTIE
He helped me with the dust.

PRESIDENT
Now he is dust, and …

DR. BROWN
… and you will be too if you don't be quiet, Mr. President.
(One of the Patients begins to throttle the PRESIDENT)

PRESIDENT
Help! I have no arms!

DR. BROWN
Get him off the President. We are not launching a revolution. This is a place of healing. I know you are all feeling down, but I know equally well you will one day feel much better, and then you will thank us for saving you.

PRESIDENT
Help!

DR. BROWN
Mr. President!

PRESIDENT
I want to go home!

GODOT
You are home.

LADY DALY
You can put your sausage you know where.

LUCILLE
Now, dears.

ALICE
Don't quibble over death. Suicide runs in the human race. Why, the twentieth century saw more butchering than the preceding ten centuries combined.

DOTTIE
What a mess.

DR. BROWN
But now we have been born again, and I hope I speak for the world in saying —

PRESIDENT
Vive le Quebec libre!

DR. BROWN
One more word, Mr. President, and we'll send you to the quiet room.
(PRESIDENT subsides)

DR. BROWN
Now, in memory of Godot...

GODOT
I want to say a prayer, in remembrance of myself —
"May the grace that
Gives life beauty,
And the love
That hallows it,
Be with us all."
(Everyone looks at GODOT)

ALICE
That was nice.

LUCILLE
Darling.
(DR. BROWN clears his throat)

DR. BROWN
Please. We know you are free of disease, as homosexuality is no longer a crime or even a mental disability. But be discreet. To continue: does anyone have anything to share with us today?

UNCLE STURTEVANT
When are we leaving?

DR. BROWN
When the world is ready for you.
(GODOT stands as if to speak, then sits perplexed)

DR. BROWN
Mr. Godot?

GODOT
If we are here, and the world is there, where am I?

PRESIDENT
A little lie might convince someone to let you out.

DR. BROWN
Mr. President, you interrupt too much and have nothing to say. Yesterday you smuggled in beer, got drunk and tried to rape a male nurse. This cannot continue.
(PRESIDENT smirks and ogles a handsome male intern)

ALICE
(To LUCILLE quietly)
How did he ever get elected?

LUCILLE
At least we are not promiscuous.

ALICE
I love you.

LUCILLE
I love you.
(PRESIDENT'S eyes begin to twitch)

DR. BROWN
(To nurse)
Get him some cogentin.

GODOT
He needs fresh air.

DOTTIE
He's too fresh as it is. He attacked me as soon as he arrived, and I am not young.

GODOT
Neither is he.

LUCILLE
He looks almost worn out.

ALICE
The job is big and he is small.
(PRESIDENT spreads his legs and screams)

PRESIDENT
Look at me!
(Everyone looks. PRESIDENT subsides)

DR. BROWN
Now…

PRESIDENT
(Interrupts)
The food here stinks.

LUCILLE
Mr. President, let's not be infantile. You will be here for a while and you will get used to it.

GODOT
I doubt it.
(PRESIDENT smirks again, then leers at everyone present)

DR. BROWN
I think that is all for today.
(BLACKOUT)

ACT II

SCENE 2 – The Outer Hebrides

        GODOT
Perhaps a little medication would help.
(PRESIDENT is writhing in his sleep on the ground)

        GODOT
Any suggestions?

        MADAME
Some more tea.

        A
Let's not overdose him.

        B
Reality is a great cure.

        GODOT
We have to bring him up gently.
(Quietly)
    Mr. President? Jack?
(PRESIDENT stops writhing)

        MADAME
Sir?

PRESIDENT
Yes?

MADAME
Are you awake?
(PRESIDENT looks around)

PRESIDENT
I thought I was mad.

A
You were.

B
Now you are saved.

PRESIDENT
How can you tell?

GODOT
Now you are awake.

MADAME
Did you have a pleasant rest?

PRESIDENT
I was in a straightjacket.

A
Really?

GODOT
Did it help?

PRESIDENT
Help?

DANIEL
It must have been a nightmare.

PRESIDENT
No worse than the White House.

DANIEL
You can get used to anything.

GODOT
Even the White House.

PRESIDENT
Am I alive?

GODOT
(With patience)
You are beyond life, and learning fast.

PRESIDENT
I don't want to learn. I know enough already.

MADAME
Of course, my dear. But don't you think a little change of mind would suit the change of scenery?

PRESIDENT
I can't change.

GODOT
You are already changing.

PRESIDENT
I don't want to change.

MADAME
That is because you love yourself too much.

B
You know what the Greeks said?

PRESIDENT
What Greeks?

B
(Slowly)
Gnothi sauton — know thyself.

PRESIDENT
How much is there to know?

GODOT
We will find out.

PRESIDENT
I don't want to know.

GODOT
Shall we put you to sleep again?
(PRESIDENT begins to shake)

B
I think he's entering recovery mode.

PRESIDENT
Recovery from what?

GODOT
Life.

A
It doesn't take long.

B
A and I have been working on it for the last two thousand years. It gave us something to do.

PRESIDENT
Two thousand years?

A
Approximately.

PRESIDENT
Maybe I am crazy.

GODOT
His mind is lifting.

  A
He is beginning to feel intelligent.

  PRESIDENT
I don't ever want to fall asleep again.

  A
(To GODOT)
Don't push things.

  GODOT
What difference does it make? He's an ex-President without a retinue.

  PRESIDENT
I am lost.

  A
You are found.

  GODOT
You are lucky to have found us.
(PRESIDENT groans)

  A
This guy will not move.

  B
Let's build a fire underneath him.

  MADAME
Mr. President, some tea with your entertainment?
(PRESIDENT groans)

  PRESIDENT
I need a drink.

  GODOT
Brandy?
(GODOT offers a bottle. PRESIDENT takes a long drink)

         A
He's retrogressing.

         B
Maybe we should put him to sleep again.
(PRESIDENT drinks again)

        GODOT
At this rate, he'll be soused before we finish the show. Mr. President…
(PRESIDENT leers)

       PRESIDENT
Yes?

        GODOT
Brandy is not beer. I'll take it back, now.

       MADAME
He's in his cups again.

        A
He was never out of them.

        GODOT
Mr. President, are you prepared for a new life?

       PRESIDENT
I don't want to go back.

        GODOT
Not back, forward.

       PRESIDENT
They were all hurting me, and I didn't know it.

        A
You were tough.

PRESIDENT
(Drinking)
   I still am.

GODOT
   I am powerless.

B
Where is Dr. Fish?

A
He went back to Vermont.

B
That's a help.
(DR. FISH enters)

DR. FISH
Here I am!

GODOT
I cannot seem to cure this one. It is the only failure of my life.
(Grand silence)

GODOT
Yes. Well, Dr. Fish, do you have a new idea?

FISH
Ignore him.

PRESIDENT
What?
(Everyone ignores this)

GODOT
A fast life can lead you to a terrifying end.

MADAME
Tea has always restored me.

PRESIDENT
Hello! Is anyone listening to me?
(PRESIDENT jumps up and down)

GODOT
Even our dreams can sometimes defeat us.

A
Look at the world.

PRESIDENT
Look at me!

A
Don't look at the world.

MADAME
I have some Earl Grey today.
(DANIEL enters)

DANIEL
Hello.

PRESIDENT
I know you.
(GODOT takes DANIEL aside)

GODOT
Just ignore him.
(To MADAME)
Earl Grey? I thought titles were on their way out.

A
They are.

B
And so are the people who hold them.

GODOT
People keep calling me Lord.

MADAME
It's redundant.

GODOT
I am no Lord, nor a Prince, nor a King of anything. I do not wrap myself in velvet and silk, nor eat off gold; nor do I live in a palace.
(GODOT gestures to the surrounding air)

GODOT
I am here with you. You are my children, and I love you, all of you.

MADAME
Have some tea.

GODOT
Thank you.

DANIEL
Mr. Godot…
(A very beautiful young woman enters and waves to DANIEL. Everyone looks at her and then to DANIEL, then they pause)

DANIEL
I have met someone new.

PRESIDENT
Road kill?
(PRESIDENT is ignored)

DANIEL
(To everyone)
Her name is Elizabeth.

LIZ
"Liz."

MADAME
I approve already.

GODOT
I have gained a daughter.

A
This is a surprise.
(To B)
I wonder if he will still love us.

B
Daniel, we bless you.

GODOT
And Liz.

MADAME
She is very beautiful.

PRESIDENT
But can she talk?

LIZ
Who is that person?

DANIEL
It doesn't matter. Mr. Godot, is it alright if I...

GODOT
Daniel, as I have already said, love has many faces.

MADAME
We will always love you.

GODOT
Yes.

A & B
We will, too.

PRESIDENT
Doesn't anyone love me?
(They all ignore him)

MADAME
Some kinds of love come cheap.

PRESIDENT
I am not cheap!
(Everyone ignores this)

DANIEL
I am glad you like Liz.

LIZ
I like your friends. I can usually judge someone by the friends they keep.

A
(To B)
She's smart, too.

B
Double lovely.

LIZ
But why so many men here?

DANIEL
It looks as though I have three fathers, and only one mother.

A
He was adopted.

B
We adopted him.

GODOT
I conceived him.

MADAME
I bore him.

DANIEL
And here I am, surrounded by love.

PRESIDENT

It will not get you anywhere!
(PRESIDENT gets up, then slips and falls into a mud puddle. Everyone continues to ignore him)

PRESIDENT

Help! Help! Help!

MADAME

Rather windy today.

GODOT

Quite a breeze.

A

I could use a nice piece of toast.

B

I need a gin and tonic.

GODOT

(Brandishing a bottle)
Brandy, anyone?
(GODOT distributes glasses and pours)

PRESIDENT

Won't anyone listen to me?
(They all continue to ignore PRESIDENT)

MADAME

(To DANIEL)
Have you read Wind In the Willows recently?

DANIEL

I never liked that one. All those talking animals.

GODOT

What about "Doctor Doolittle?"

A
My doctors never did much for me.

B
Doctors… Dentists are the worst. I think those x-rays must have been what brought on the cancer.

PRESIDENT
(Desperately)
Cancer?

MADAME
We all die, even of cancer.

GODOT
Some of us die of presumption.

B
Some of us die of other people's presumption.

PRESIDENT
Look at me!
(All continue to studiously ignore him)

LIZ
How is life in the Outer Hebrides? I have never been here before.

A
You will get used to it.

B
(Quietly)
Should I tell her?

DANIEL
That is my job. Liz, you are dead. All of us are dead.

LIZ
Things seem the same. You feel solid. I can smell your hair. Your lips are keen to kiss. And there is a lot more of you that I hope to explore.

DANIEL
You will. But we are dead.

LIZ
Then I guess we don't need to get married. The economic question has been solved.

DANIEL
In more ways than you might think.

PRESIDENT
I will make you Secretary of the Treasury. I can make you all anything I want!

DANIEL
Liz, death offers you all the things life didn't: even love.

LIZ
I died for love.

GODOT
Don't go into that now, dear. There is plenty of time later to swap histories.

DANIEL
I am not interested in your history, Liz, only your present and our future.

A
Now he's gushing.

B
Love.

PRESIDENT
I am not gushing.
(The PRESIDENT is beginning to go mad)
PRESIDENT
I never gush. I love my aides. I love everyone. And the whole world loves me back. I am giving them all their freedom. That is the best I can do, as President.

MADAME
We seem to have run out of tea.

B
Anyone for coffee?

MADAME
But coffee is the drink of death.

A
Yes.

GODOT
Let us offer some to the President. Jack! You want something to drink?

PRESIDENT
(Slobbering)
Coffee? It will keep me awake.

GODOT
We don't want to interfere with your dreams.

MADAME
Any of them…

B
Have a nice cup of coffee. It will put you to sleep.

MADAME
He has put many people to sleep.

GODOT
It goes with the job.

DANIEL
Not at all. His predecessor fought wars without firing a shot.

GODOT
I knew him.
(There is silence)

GODOT
Ah, well. We are all human.

PRESIDENT
Reckless sinner!
(Everyone raises their eyebrows)

MADAME
Coffee, tea or milk?

A
Do you have anything solid to offer?

MADAME
We have a few stale scones. I made them myself.
(A tries one)

A
Very stale.

GODOT
I have told you, food is unnecessary here.

MADAME
But it still ranks as a superfluous pleasure.

PRESIDENT
Where is my pleasure?

GODOT
I wish Professor Fish were here. He would give us the right diagnosis.

B
I think he is depressed - and rapidly descending into paranoia.

MADAME
Maybe a little conversational therapy.

GODOT
He must help himself: that is the Conservative doctrine.

A
The Conservatives can be so doctrinaire.

B
And contradictory.

A
And hypocritical.

GODOT
Take the President -

PRESIDENT
Don't take me anywhere!

GODOT
You see. He has suddenly found his home.

MADAME
But he is mad.

GODOT
He was mad. Now he is waking up - to tea.

MADAME
Here.
(PRESIDENT cringes)

GODOT
Do not touch him yet. He is very sensitive.

A
I wonder if he made scenes like this in the White House?

B
Probably.

A
There he got away with it.

B
He was President.

PRESIDENT
Now I am dead.

GODOT
I told you so.

PRESIDENT
Who?

GODOT
The others didn't think I could salvage you.

PRESIDENT
Salvage?

GODOT
All souls are equal, once they die. So I knew I could help. You were just carrying a lot of baggage.

PRESIDENT
I can carry my own baggage.

GODOT
That's a start.

A
Start?

B
Quiet!

PRESIDENT
I will write you all into my will.

A
He's relapsing.

GODOT
As I said, this one is going to require unusual effort.

A
Look! A snake!
(PRESIDENT screams)

B
Where do we go now?

A
Uphill and down dale.

MADAME
Recoveries can take ages. It all depends on what you eat. Or drink.

PRESIDENT
Potato chips and a hamburger!

MADAME
At least he enjoys thinking about food.

GODOT
It will only give him the trots.

A
That is another start.

GODOT
You are beginning to understand my methods.

B
This is cruel.

GODOT
It is the only way I have discovered to squeeze out the evil in such people. It is hardly anything when compared to the pains they have brought to others.

A
I guess I am just soft on sin.

B
You are a Democrat.

A
And Godot is…?

B
I think Godot is realistic.

GODOT
My methods have so far worked with everyone you know.

B
We know.

A
I am still a Democrat.

B
I don't think Godot is either a Democrat or a Republican.
(GODOT smiles)

GODOT
You are all my children.

A
I once heard the Archbishop of Canterbury say that.

B
He had children?

A
He said, "We are all God's children."

B
Godot's.

A
Godot's.

GODOT
Yes. That particular Archbishop hadn't heard of me.

A
Now he has.

B
Now they all have.

A
Even us, in the Outer Hebrides.

B
What a joy!

A
(To GODOT)
You do offer us some comfort.
(A begins to cry. PRESIDENT begins to wail)

B
So this is how it goes. How long is he (pointing to President) going to take?

GODOT
I don't know. The wound is pretty deep.

MADAME
There is a lot of rot inside.

GODOT
I cannot use my usual tools. I think another dream might help.

A
We weren't privy to the last one.

GODOT
I was, in one of my many capacities.

B
You were in his dream?

GODOT
It helps if you pay attention to the patient.

A
Whoa!

B
So they call him Godot…

A
Let's watch the dream.
(Lights dim. Two screens descend again. More speeches, scenes of war, etc. We are in the Oval Office. AIDES 1 and 2, DOTTIE and LADY DALY come in and out)

AIDE 1
Where is the President?

AIDE 2
Powdering his nose.

AIDE 1
We have orders for the War.

AIDE 2
The usual.

AIDE 1
The usual war?

AIDE 2
Shh. He's coming.
(Enter current President – LANCELOT BROWN)

BROWN
What's on the menu?

AIDE 1
More signatures. Orders for the War.

BROWN
How many casualties today - on our side?

AIDE 2
Two.

BROWN
The usual. Where do I sign?
(BROWN signs)

PRESIDENT
But it's my war! I want it back!

GODOT
Be quiet. They can't hear you.

BROWN
What's for lunch?

AIDE 2
Health care.

BROWN
I'm not joking.

AIDE 1
I'll go see.
(AIDE 1 exits. BROWN studies ceiling)

AIDE 2
Fine day.

BROWN
I am playing golf this afternoon.
(Pausing)
With my contributors. Suckers.

AIDE 2
Yes sir.

AIDE 1

Choice of veal stew or meatloaf.

BROWN

Anything in the stew?

AIDE 1

I'll ask.

(AIDE 1 exits)

BROWN

Fine day.

AIDE 2

Very fine.

BROWN

It's a little boring here today. Shall we cook up another war? Protect the homeland? Get those creeps?

AIDE 2

Sir?

BROWN

I shoot very high. One war down, another to go.

AIDE 2

Yessir.

BROWN

Do you shoot?

AIDE 2

Excuse me, Sir?

BROWN

Do you hunt? Game?

AIDE 2

Game? A game?

BROWN
You know, deer, bear, elk?

AIDE 2
I haven't tried it, Sir. My husband would object.

BROWN
Great sport. Hunting them down.

AIDE 2
People?

BROWN
Animals. People are animals.

AIDE 2
Animals are people. Or so my daughter tells me.

BROWN
I didn't know you had one.

AIDE 2
One daughter.

BROWN
How old is she?

AIDE 2
Eight.

BROWN
Eight?

AIDE 2
Going to be nine in three days.

BROWN
Children…
(AIDE 1 re-enters)

AIDE 1
The stew is veal à l'Ancienne, with onions, mushrooms and Béchamel sauce.

BROWN
I'll have the meatloaf. My wife calls me pedestrian.

AIDE 1
Yessir.

AIDE 2
Yessir.

BROWN
Nonsense. She's just joking. Very pedestrian.

AIDE 1
Yes, Mr. President.
(PRESIDENT still is shadows next to GODOT)

PRESIDENT
I am usurped.

GODOT
They can't hear you.

PRESIDENT
Look at me!
(The others are oblivious)

GODOT
They don't remember you.
(PRESIDENT emits strangled sound)

BROWN
Life is hard. So much work.
(BROWN takes an apple off a desk and begins to eat it)

BROWN
So, what's next?

AIDE 1
It's one of your free days, Mr. President.

BROWN
I'll go work out.

AIDE 1
Yessir.

AIDE 2
Yessir.
(BROWN and AIDES exit)

PRESIDENT
No one listens any more.

GODOT
I am listening.

PRESIDENT
Could we talk?
(GODOT sits behind desk)

GODOT
(Getting up)
This is your place.

PRESIDENT
I resign.

GODOT
I accept.

PRESIDENT
Is this all that's left?

GODOT
An empty chair. An empty room.

PRESIDENT
They didn't even see me…

GODOT
They never will again.

PRESIDENT
But I still see myself.

GODOT
Now you do.
(PRESIDENT begins to cry)

GODOT
Tissue?
(GODOT hands PRESIDENT a hanky)

PRESIDENT
Thank you.

GODOT
A small favor for a big man.

PRESIDENT
But I'm not big anymore.

GODOT
You have just begun to be big.

PRESIDENT
But what can I do if I'm dead? I have no influence. They don't even know I'm here.

GODOT
Let's go back to your new friends. They may have an idea what to do.
(GODOT takes PRESIDENT by the shoulder and gently guides him out the door)
(SLOW FADE)

ACT III

SCENE 1

LADY DALY enters with PRESIDENT.

    LADY DALY
We would like to help you, if we could.

    PRESIDENT
But we're all dead.

    GODOT
A small problem.

    A
What do dead people do?

    GODOT
Some say the good ones become angels.

    DOTTIE
But we are all good, now that we are cured.

    PRESIDENT
Cured of life…

    GODOT
Yes. And so the ranks of angels are always growing.

    A
But what do we do?

GODOT
You may stay here in the Outer Hebrides and drink tea, or you may jump off my famous cliff and authorize yourselves for another journey, or you may decamp to any part of the world and adopt a new role in life.

PRESIDENT
The transmigration of souls.

A
Where did he pick up that one?

B
Knowledge blooms in Godot's company.

A
So does love.

LADY DALY
I heard that.

GODOT
You are all correct. But you must make your choices, and the present is certainly a good time to begin —

PRESIDENT
— Again.

LADY DALY
(To PRESIDENT)
You have seen us in the White House.

PRESIDENT
Wasn't my replacement your husband?

LADY DALY
He was my husband. Now he's my boss.

A
Flip-flop.

GODOT
He was ready for the job.

PRESIDENT
This is extraordinary. But if Mr. Brown has taken my place, how do I get back?

GODOT
There are many roles in the world, as many as there are people. You can cast yourself however you wish, but you cannot come back as your former self. Can you think of anything that would interest you?

PRESIDENT
I've already been top man. How about Minister Plenipotentiary?

GODOT
How about Private Counselor?

PRESIDENT
I get no publicity? Where's the fun in that?

GODOT
That's where all the fun is. Trust me. It's my job.

PRESIDENT
Will you come with me?

GODOT
I'm a trouper, and I will be happy to help.

PRESDIENT
When do we begin? What do I wear?

GODOT
We begin as soon as possible. You ought to know what to wear.

PRESIDENT
I'll wear my favorite blue suit and my Hermes red tie.

GODOT

A little free publicity can always be helpful, as long as the product merits the praise.

PRESIDENT

Oooh, ooh. I'm excited.

GODOT

Don't get too excited. The world is a big mess. In your previous incarnation, you chose some ruinous policies.

PRESIDENT

I had to get re-elected.

GODOT

We all have to get re-elected, every day of our lives. Off with you!

(PRESIDENT and GODOT exit)

ACT III

SCENE 2

PRESIDENT
Doing nothing is very hard.
(Pausing)
I hope I can find something to do with eternity.

GODOT
That is my problem exactly. What to do?

PRESIDENT
Any answers?

GODOT
Make friends. Influence people.

PRESIDENT
But that is what I have been doing.

GODOT
On the wrong side of the mirror. Reverse yourself. Turn your life — your death — around.

PRESIDENT
I don't understand.

GODOT
Think of life and death as an example of matter and anti-matter.

PRESIDENT
Anti-matter?

GODOT
In physics, half of reality is missing. That is anti-matter. Some people think of it as black matter — as though it were invisible. It is not invisible. It is perceptible. It is what drives poets and seers. Think of Nature. Think of the Greeks. Think of all the Gods and Heroes. Think of them. Think of them and where they have gone now.

PRESIDENT
Not here.

GODOT
Wrong. You will meet your peers here soon enough. And some have chosen to live in the world. Int he world you have just left.

PRESIDENT
It has left me.

GODOT
Yes.

PRESIDENT
So what do we do?

GODOT
What do we ever do?

PRESIDENT
Become catatonic?

GODOT
That is what happens when you begin to discover the half of reality that you never knew.

PRESIDENT
I know.

GODOT
That discovery is very dangerous, and many do not survive. Others end up living their lives in a kind of excruciating twilight — caught between two worlds and never able to choose between them.

PRESIDENT
Here I am.

GODOT
Yes, you are here. Some more tea?

PRESIDENT
Is all that's left talking in the Outer Hebrides?

GODOT
Of course not. Consider yourself a soul on a journey to an infinity number of new worlds.

PRESIDENT
Will I always be alone?

GODOT
No. You have already met some companions, if you want them. If not, there are many more. Death has been at work for an eternity.

PRESIDENT
You are smart.

GODOT
You don't believe me?

PRESIDENT
I take you on faith.

GODOT
I am giving you the facts, and you will know that very soon. In the meantime, you may accept what I say however you wish. As for faith, I am not a great fan of being foolish. Anything can

be accepted as faith — people accept whole lifetimes on faith, and look what happens! Faith is a crutch and it holds nothing up except ignorance. You may dress yourself in faith. I do not.

PRESIDENT
You mean —

GODOT
I, too, am faced with the problem.

PRESIDENT
Me, too.
(They smile and exchange a non-voluptuous kiss)

PRESIDENT
So there really is love in Heaven.

GODOT
You are still in the Outer Hebrides, and Heaven is everywhere, even on Earth.

PRESIDENT
What about sex?

GODOT
It is simply the embodiment of love. And sometimes love is confused with lust.

PRESIDENT
I was hoping for a little lust in the other life.

GODOT
You can have it.

PRESIDENT
Oh.

GODOT
People generally die old, and if they do, they don't have much further use for lust. Like various types of food, it offers pleasure, nothing more.

PRESIDENT
What about procreation?

GODOT
I shall have to save that for another time. I see someone coming.

ACT III

SCENE 3

      A
I smell smoke.

      B
It must be the tea.

      A
Something is burning.

      B
Your brain or mine?
(A sees GODOT and PRESIDENT)

      A
O! The culprits. Are you overheating?

      PRESIDENT
We were just conversing.

      A
Ah. Did the words stick?

      GODOT
Jack makes a fine student.

      PRESIDENT
It is my new role in life — in death.

B
We are moving.

PRESIDENT
Moving?

A
We think two thousand years on the heath are enough.

B
We are at a jumping-off point.

A
We have come to a conclusion.

B
We are tired of being alone together.

A
So we are going South.

PRESIDENT
South?

A
To the cliff.

PRESIDENT
After such a short acquaintance?

B
You are not the only President in the universe.

A
We are jumping off the famous cliff.

B
All we needed was a little courage.

A
After two thousand years, we have gathered all the courage we need, and now we are ready to proceed into the unknown.

>   B
> The next phase.

>   GODOT
> The illimitable...

>   A
> *(To PRESIDENT)*
> Nice to meet you.

>   B
> Yes.

>   GODOT
> You need a witness.

>   PRESIDENT
> Maybe we should have a jumping-off party.

>   GODOT
> Good idea!

>   B
> We don't need company.

>   A
> No.

>   PRESIDENT
> Of course you do. We all hope to follow your example, sooner or later.

>   A
> Alright. But don't take too long preparing.

>   B
> We don't want to lose our resolve.

>   A
> Art lives on self-discovery, and the art of life does too.

B
We are about to discover ourselves anew.

A
I wish I had a horn. We need a little advertisement if we are going to have a party.

B
Here.

A
Where did that come from?

B
(Pointing to GODOT)
Ask him.
(GODOT smiles)

A
Semper paratus.

GODOT
In one of my many incarnations...

A
(Interrupting)
...yes, we know.
(He blows the horn. DOTTIE, LADY DALY, BROWN and the rest appear. Lights go down. Lights up at the edge of the cliff. The cast are all standing around as at a cocktail party, with drinks, hors d'oeuvres, etc. Everyone is chatting pleasantly)

LUCILLE
This is the best cocktail I have ever tasted.

ALICE
The bartender is over there. He arrived just yesterday.
(To BARTENDER)
Antonio! Antonio!
(BARTENDER comes over)

ALICE
Lucille says this is a fabulous drink.

LUCILLE
The best I ever tasted.

ALICE
She is an expert.

LUCILLE
A connoisseur.

ANTONIO
(Smiling)
It is my job.
(He bows formally and attends to the others)

DOTTIE
No dust here.

LADY DALY
Solid rock.

BROWN
Am I dead again?
(Pauses)
I rather enjoyed being President.

LADY DALY
A suicide bomber blew you up, along with the West Wing.

BROWN
I don't see the suicide bomber.

GODOT
I have reduced him to nothing.
(There is silence)

A
How do we know this is going to work?

> B

We don't want to end up as nothing.

> PRESIDENT

(Looking at GODOT)
I think you have to take what he says on faith.
(GODOT shrugs)

> GODOT

I have told you what I know.

> A

Oh.

> B

Oh.

> A

Well, I am prepared to jump in any case.

> B

Two thousand years on the heath are enough.

> A

Another cocktail?

> B

Let's go.
(They shake hands and wave to the others. They approach the abyss, then jump. Everyone gasps. Two flashes of light shoot up into the sky. There is a tremendous clap of thunder. The light recedes)

> DOTTIE

That was fun.

> LADY DALY

I wonder if it hurts.

> GODOT

Not at all. It is my preferred method of getting from one venue to the next. And now it is my turn.

(GODOT jumps. Everyone gasps)

          LUCILLE
That was novel.

          DOTTIE
Yes.

(All present begin to look at each other with the same idea in mind)

          DOTTIE
Are you ready?

(They all nod. All jump off the cliff. Fireworks ensue)

—FINIS—

www.ingramcontent.com/pod-product-compliance
Lightning Source LLC
Chambersburg PA
CBHW030158100526
44592CB00009B/343